My Spelling Workbook

This book belongs to:

....

My Spelling Workbook *(Book C)*

Published by Prim-Ed Publishing 2011
3rd edition 2021
Reprinted 2015, 2021
Copyright© Prim-Ed Publishing 2011
ISBN 978-1-80087-110-6
PR–2282

Titles available in this series:
My Spelling Workbook *(Book A)*
My Spelling Workbook *(Book B)*
My Spelling Workbook *(Book C)*
My Spelling Workbook *(Book D)*
My Spelling Workbook *(Book E)*
My Spelling Workbook *(Book F)*
My Spelling Workbook *(Book G)*

Copyright Notice

No part of this book may be reproduced in any form or by any means, electronic or mechanical, including photocopying or recording, or by an information retrieval system without written permission from the publisher.

Offices in:
UK and Republic of Ireland:
Marshmeadows
New Ross
County Wexford
www.prim-ed.com

Australia:
PO Box 332
Greenwood
Western Australia 6924
www.ricpublications.com.au

Introduction

Welcome to **My Spelling Workbook**.
This book and interactive download have lots of activities to help you learn to spell.
You should follow this method when you are learning to spell each word.

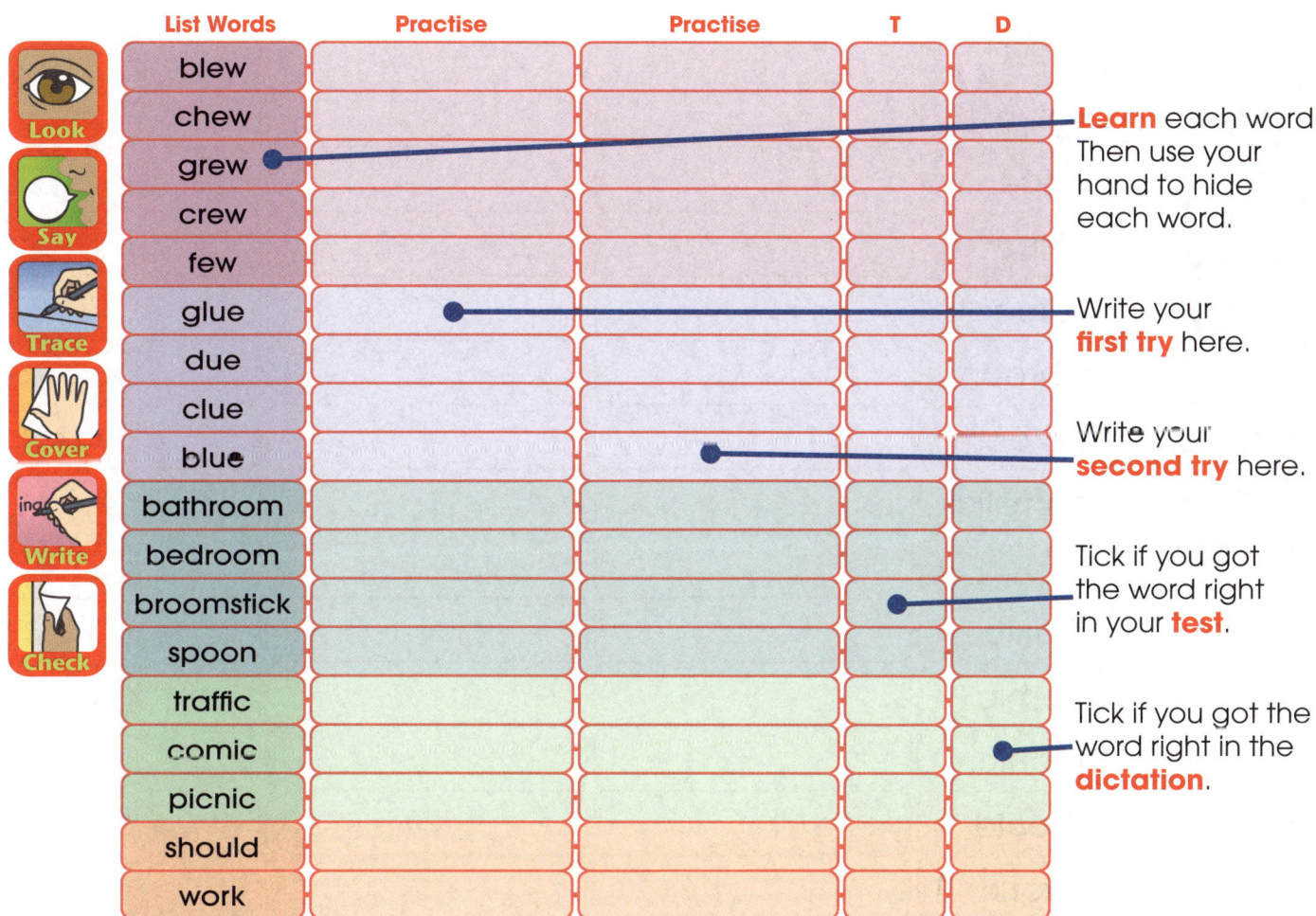

Contents

Unit 1 *ew, ue, oo, ic* 2–5	Unit 11 *ge, dge, ch, tch* 42–45
Unit 2 *o saying u, -ck* 6–9	Unit 12 *Compound Words* 46–49
Unit 3 *nk, i-e, y, ie, igh* 10–13	Unit 13 *Spring/Easter* 50–53
Unit 4 *ll, ss, zz, ff* 14–17	Unit 14 *Contractions* 54–57
Unit 5 *le* 18–21	Unit 15 *aw, oa, ore, a* 58–61
Unit 6 *scr, spr, str* 22–25	Unit 16 *war* 62–65
Unit 7 *Christmas* 26–29	Unit 17 *Silent Letters* 66–69
Unit 8 *qu, squ* 30–33	Unit 18 *Summer Holidays* 70–73
Unit 9 *old, ind* 34–37	Difficult Words I Have Found 74
Unit 10 *ice, ace* 38–41	My Spelling Dictionary Aa–Zz 75–78

My Spelling Workbook C—Prim-Ed Publishing—www.prim-ed.com

Unit 1

	List Words	Practise	Practise	T	D
 Look	blew 1				
	chew				
 Say	grew 10				
	crew				
 Trace	few 2				
	glue				
 Cover	due				
	clue 3				
 Write	blue 4				
	bathroom 5				
	bedroom 6				
 Check	broomstick				
	spoon 7				
	traffic 8				
	comic				
	picnic				
	should				
	work 9				

Picture Matching

1. Write the list word that matches each picture.

   (a)

   (b)

   (c)

   (d)

Missing Letters

2. Complete these list words.

   (a) br ___ ___ mst ___ ck

   (b) ___ ___ ___ ff ___ ___

   (c) ___ e ___

   (d) sh ___ ___ d

   (e) s ___ o ___ n

   (f) b ___ t ___ ___ om

Unit 1

Crossword

3. Use list words to solve the crossword.

Across

1. A small number.
3. Lots of moving vehicles.
5. The wind ___ all night.
6. A knife, fork and ___.
7. A room with a bath.
8. It is used to stick things together.
10. Got larger, taller or bigger.
12. To bite or munch food.
13. A child's picture magazine.
15. Expected at certain times.

Down

2. My dad goes to ___ at 7 am.
4. It is a help to solve a problem.
5. A witch flies on one.
6. I know I ___ always be good.
7. A room for sleeping in.
9. A colour that rhymes with 'clue'.
11. A packed meal eaten outdoors.
14. The workers on a ship.

Secret Code

4. Use the secret code to find the list word.

(a) ___ ___ ___
    (3) (2) (10)

(b) ___ ___ ___ ___
    (10) (7) (8) (5)

(c) ___ ___ ___ ___
    (1) (6) (9) (2)

(d) ___ ___ ___ ___
    (4) (8) (2) (10)

b	1
e	2
f	3
g	4
k	5
l	6
o	7
r	8
u	9
w	10

Word Challenge

5. Make as many words as you can from the letters in this word.

bathroom

Unit 1

List Words

- blew
- chew
- grew
- crew
- few
- glue
- due
- clue
- blue
- bathroom
- bedroom
- broomstick
- spoon
- traffic
- comic
- picnic
- should
- work

Revision Words

- shoe
- shut
- short
- fresh
- brush
- wish
- two
- three

Proofreading

6. Circle the incorrect words and rewrite them correctly in the spaces.

(a) You shoold clean your blew shoos for wurk.
_____

(b) Too of the crue are on a picknick.
_____

Missing Words

7. Complete the sentences using one of the list or revision words.

(a) My train is _____ at five o'clock.

(b) The plane and its _____ flew out an hour ago.

(c) Help your sister _____ her hair.

(d) The police directed the _____.

Shape Sorter

8. Write the word that fits in each shape.

(a)

(b)

(c)

Compound Words

9. Match the words to make compound words.

| cut | room | stick |

(a) bed_____

(b) broom_____

(c) bath_____

(d) short_____

Unit 1

Word Search

10. Find the list and revision words in the word search.

blew	due	broomstick
chew	clue	spoon
grew	blue	traffic
crew	bathroom	comic
few	bedroom	picnic
glue	work	should
shoe	shut	short
fresh	brush	wish
two	three	

t	s	h	o	e	l	n	v	g	g	l	u	e
w	d	t	b	r	o	o	m	s	t	i	c	k
o	u	r	r	g	r	e	w	v	r	t	l	g
i	e	a	u	s	h	u	t	h	r	e	e	l
r	s	f	s	p	i	c	n	i	c	e	s	j
g	p	f	h	c	l	u	e	j	l	q	w	c
s	o	i	t	m	z	y	d	b	l	u	e	o
h	o	c	n	b	o	b	e	d	r	o	o	m
o	n	w	o	r	k	s	h	o	u	l	d	i
r	b	a	t	h	r	o	o	m	w	o	c	c
t	p	t	v	u	f	r	e	s	h	a	h	a
v	c	r	e	w	g	c	x	l	z	f	e	w
q	n	z	w	i	s	h	c	b	l	e	w	q

Synonyms

11. Find list or revision words with similar meanings.

(a) funny _____   (b) closed _____

(c) job _____   (d) team _____

(e) chomp _____   (f) must _____

What am I?

12. (a) I am enjoyable.
I am packaged in a bag.
I include food and drink.
You usually eat me outdoors.

I am a ☐ .

(b) I come in different colours.
I come in pairs.
I have a sole.

I am a ☐ .

Additional Activities

13. (a) Write six more '**colour**' words. Check your spelling.

(b) Write your new colour words in alphabetical order.

(c) For each colour word, write a list of four objects that are usually this colour.

Unit 2

o saying u   -ck

 Look
 Say
 Trace
 Cover
 Write
 Check

List Words	Practise	Practise	T	D
love 1				
above 9				
oven 2				
cover				
mother 3				
brother				
another 4				
other				
Monday 5				
front				
onion 6				
back				
trick 7				
brick				
shock 8				
luck				
Ireland 10				
March				

Antonyms

Antonyms are words with the opposite meaning. '**Hot**' and '**cold**' are antonyms.

1. Find a list word with the opposite meaning.

   (a) father _____

   (b) below _____

   (c) hate _____

   (d) sister _____

Word Maker

2. Join '**ck**' to the end of the letters in the circles to make new words.

Unit 2

o saying u **-ck**

Crossword

3. Use list words to solve the crossword.

Across
2. One more.
4. A vegetable.
5. Opposite of front.
7. To adore.
9. Third month of the year.
11. I saw him the ___ day.
12. A country beginning with 'I'.
14. It is used in building.
15. Opposite of father.
16. Over.

Down
1. You cook in this.
3. I can do a good card ___.
6. A lid, top or cap.
8. She touched the wire and got a ___.
9. Day before Tuesday.
10. Opposite of back.
13. We wished him ___ in his test.
14. Opposite of sister.

Word Worm

5. Circle each list word you can find in the word worm.

Syllables

4. Add the missing syllable to finish the list word.

(a) o + ther ▶▶▶
(b) a + ▶▶▶
(c) Ire + ▶▶▶
(d) mo + ▶▶▶
(e) Mon + ▶▶▶

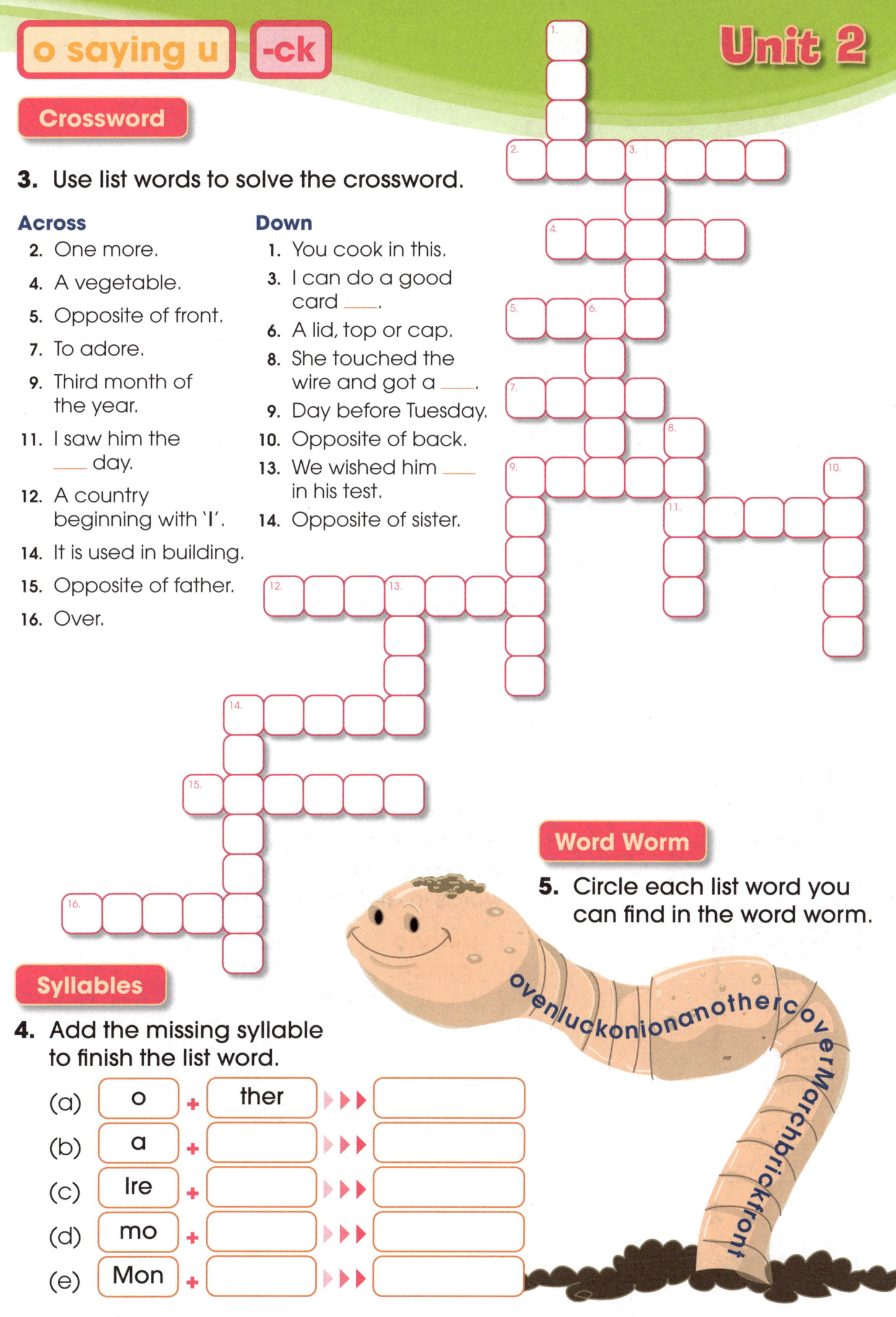

My Spelling Workbook C—Prim-Ed Publishing—www.prim-ed.com

Unit 2

o saying u **-ck**

List Words

- love
- above
- oven
- cover
- mother
- brother
- another
- other
- Monday
- front
- onion
- back
- trick
- brick
- shock
- luck
- Ireland
- March

Revision Words

- such
- chin
- chip
- lunch
- punch
- church
- four
- five

Word Hunt

6. (a) Which list words have the same five letters?

☐ ☐
☐ ☐

(b) Which list words start with a capital letter?

☐ ☐ ☐

(c) Which list word is in the word 'glove'?

☐

Plurals

7. Add 's' or 'es' to make these words plural.

(a) mother ☐ (b) church ☐
(c) lunch ☐ (d) shock ☐
(e) onion ☐ (f) trick ☐

Alphabetical Order

8. Write these list and revision words in alphabetical order.

Ireland   back
punch   oven
       cover

_____
_____
_____
_____
_____

Unit 2

o saying u **-ck**

Word Search

9. Find the list and revision words in the word search.

love	another	trick
above	other	brick
oven	Monday	shock
cover	front	luck
mother	onion	Ireland
brother	back	March
such	chin	chip
lunch	punch	church
four	five	

u	l	a	o	n	i	o	n	l	u	c	k	a
e	u	o	f	t	x	l	s	h	o	c	k	g
a	n	t	g	o	l	o	y	f	r	o	n	t
b	c	h	c	M	r	v	u	i	c	h	i	p
o	h	e	h	o	e	e	j	t	r	i	c	k
v	n	r	u	n	l	b	s	c	o	v	e	r
e	w	c	r	d	a	r	k	p	u	n	c	h
b	b	c	c	a	n	o	t	h	e	r	y	d
b	r	h	h	y	d	t	s	u	c	h	j	a
a	i	i	e	r	y	h	i	f	i	v	e	o
c	c	n	j	m	i	e	m	o	t	h	e	r
k	k	m	f	o	u	r	a	l	t	x	t	d
b	g	w	M	a	r	c	h	y	o	v	e	n

All Mixed Up

10. Unjumble these list and revision words.

   (a) cshu _____   (b) cbirk _____

   (c) nooni _____   (d) hroatne _____

   (e) rfuo _____   (f) rotherb _____

Magic Words

11. Change the first word into the last word by changing one letter on each line to make a new word.

e.g. pack → peck → peak → beak

(a) love → ___ → ___ → post

(b) back → ___ → ___ → peak

Additional Activities

12. (a) Write five more words that end in 'ck'. Check your spelling.

   (b) Use a dictionary to write a definition for each of your new 'ck' words.

   (c) Write five sentences, each containing one of your new 'ck' words.

Unit 3

List Words	Practise	Practise	T	D
think 1				
thank 2				
sunk				
plank				
fine 3				
alive 8				
line				
reply 4				
supply				
apply				
fried 5				
tried				
cried 9				
high 6				
sigh				
right 7				
while 10				
which				

Missing Vowels

1. Write 'a', 'e', 'i' or 'u' to make list words.

   (a) fr ___ d
   (b) ___ pply
   (c) s ___ nk
   (d) wh ___ l ___
   (e) s ___ gh
   (f) l ___ n

Synonyms

2. Find a list word with a similar meaning.

   (a) answer _____
   (b) board _____
   (c) living _____
   (d) correct _____
   (e) provide _____

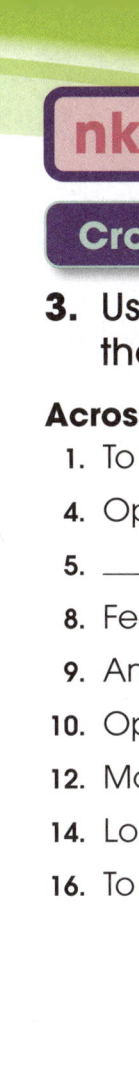 

Crossword

3. Use list words to solve the crossword.

Across
1. To believe or imagine.
4. Opposite of wrong.
5. ___ one do you prefer?
8. Feeling well.
9. Answer.
10. Opposite of dead.
12. Made an effort to do something.
14. Long flat piece of wood.
16. To provide.

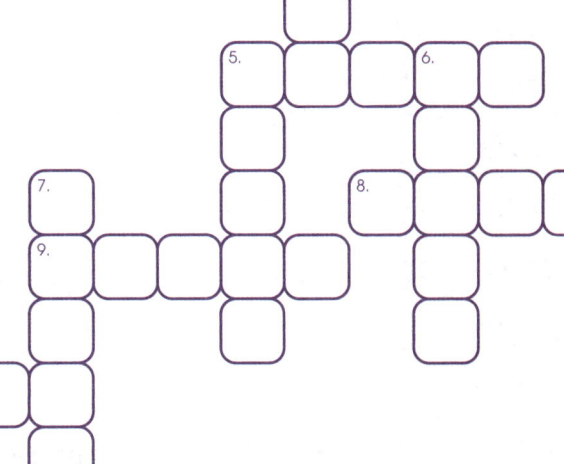

Down
2. Opposite of low.
3. He let out a ___ when the exam was over.
5. During.
6. Shed tears.
7. Cooked in hot oil.
11. I tried to write along the   .
12. ___ you for coming to my party.
13. To put to use.
15. The pirate ship was ___.

Read and Draw

4. (a) A pirate who is alive after he has walked the plank.

(b) A man who cried because he fried onions.

Unit 3

  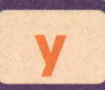 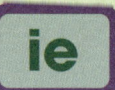 

List Words

think
thank
sunk
plank
fine
alive
line
reply
supply
apply
fried
tried
cried
high
sigh
right
while
which

Revision Words

these
them
tooth
bath
it's
I'll
only
one

Proofreading

5. Circle the incorrect words and rewrite them correctly in the spaces.

(a) He gave a sy as he tryed but failed to score a goal.

(b) I'll be fin whaisle you are away.

(c) Witch is the write path?

Changing the Tense

6. Change the words to the past or present tense.

Past tense	Present tense
	supply
cried	
fried	

Antonyms

7. Find a list word with the opposite meaning.

(a) laughed _____ (b) low _____

(c) dead _____ (d) unwell _____

(e) wrong _____

Magic Words

8. Change the first word into the last word by changing one letter on each line to make a new word.

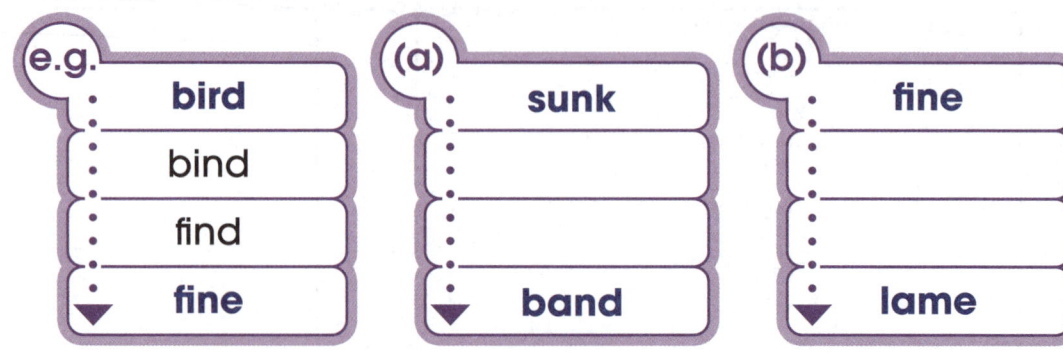

Unit 3

Word Search

9. Find the list and revision words in the word search.

think	line	cried
thank	reply	high
sunk	supply	sigh
plank	apply	right
fine	fried	while
alive	tried	which
these	them	tooth
bath	it's	I'll
only	one	

```
e g o u w h i c h y e x i
t x n a s u p p l y t I' i
h c e l w v h i g h h l j
a r i i n w w h i l e l p
n i a v r r e p l y s b l
k e p e i i t' s z t e m a
p d p c g h l z k r f a n
u k l x h o n l y i r t k
x m y d t h i n k e i b r
m t o o t h y b o d e a e
t h e m f i n e z s d t a
e s u n k v z t s i g h m
t e g b m l i n e y z p k
```

Rhyming Words

10. Choose a rhyming word from your list or revision words.

(a) path _____
(b) five _____
(c) rich _____
(d) sink _____
(e) please _____
(f) night _____

Secret Code

11. Use the secret code to find the list or revision word.

(a) ___ ___ ___ ___
   (2) (1) (10) (4)

(b) ___ ___ ___ ___ ___
   (1) (7) (5) (11) (3)

(c) ___ ___ ___ ___ ___
   (1) (9) (9) (7) (12)

(d) ___ ___ ___ ___ ___
   (9) (7) (1) (8) (6)

a	1
b	2
e	3
h	4
i	5
k	6
l	7
n	8
p	9
t	10
v	11
y	12

Additional Activities

12. (a) Write five more words that end in 'nk'.

(b) Write your new words in alphabetical order.

(c) Write five sentences, each containing one of your new 'nk' words.

Unit 4

List Words	Practise	Practise	T	D
still				
smell				
skull				
stall				
across				
dress				
glass				
miss				
jazz				
buzz				
fizz				
dizzy				
cuff				
staff				
cliff				
stuff				
yesterday				
April				

Small Words

1. Find smaller words in these words.

   (a) stall _____

   (b) miss _____

   (c) still _____

   (d) cliff _____

   (e) smell _____

Antonyms

2. Find a list word with the opposite meaning.

   (a) today

   (b) hit

   (c) moving

   (d) strip

Unit 4

ll ss zz ff

Crossword

3. Use list words to solve the crossword.

Across

3. Not moving.
5. The end part of your sleeve.
7. Feeling of your head spinning.
8. A type of music.
11. The day before today.
15. A scent or odour.
16. Fail to hit or reach something.
17. A stand for the sale of goods.
18. Things, objects or articles.

Down

1. A spring month.
2. The workers.
4. To make a humming noise.
6. Bubbles of gas in a liquid.
9. From one side to another.
10. To put on clothes.
12. The bones around a head.
13. A steep rock face.
14. Windows are mostly made of ___.

Synonyms

4. Find a list word with a similar meaning.

(a) wobbly _____
(b) bubble _____
(c) hum _____
(d) stink _____
(e) things _____

Word Challenge

5. Make as many words as you can from the letters in this word.

yesterday

Unit 4

ll ss zz ff

List Words

still
smell
skull
stall
across
dress
glass
miss
jazz
buzz
fizz
dizzy
cuff
staff
cliff
stuff
yesterday
April

Revision Words

around
house
now
down
why
where
May
many

Homographs

The word 'dress' is a homograph. This means that it has two meanings. One meaning is a verb – a doing word; the second is a noun – a naming word.

6. Write one sentence using 'dress' as a verb and one using it as a noun.

   (a) _____

   (b) _____

Guess the Word

7. Write list words to match the clues.

   (a) Bees do this.   _____

   (b) Protects your brain.   _____

   (c) Rhymes with 'will'.   _____

   (d) Girls wear this.   _____

Word Hunt

8. (a) Which list or revision words have the letter 'm'?

   (b) Which revision word rhymes with 'mouse'?

   (c) Which list words begin with 'st'?

Unit 4

ll **ss** **zz** **ff**

Word Search

9. Find the list and revision words in the word search.

still	glass	cuff
smell	miss	staff
skull	jazz	cliff
stall	buzz	stuff
across	fizz	yesterday
dress	dizzy	April
around	house	now
down	why	where
May	many	

w	h	y	s	t	i	l	l	y	h	d	m	l
s	l	s	d	w	g	A	g	e	n	m	e	j
t	l	c	v	g	c	p	r	s	t	a	l	l
u	d	i	z	z	y	r	s	t	a	f	f	c
f	d	o	w	n	h	i	k	e	b	l	n	d
f	b	u	z	z	o	l	q	r	i	x	x	r
k	m	a	n	y	u	f	d	d	p	v	a	e
a	c	r	o	s	s	g	l	a	s	s	r	s
j	s	p	w	h	e	r	e	y	q	f	o	s
a	k	p	M	a	y	c	u	f	f	i	u	p
z	u	s	a	k	u	p	o	k	b	z	n	v
z	l	s	m	e	l	l	x	z	m	z	d	u
c	l	i	f	f	e	n	o	w	m	i	s	s

Missing Letters

10. Complete these list and revision words.

(a) di __ z __ (b) w __ e __ e

(c) __ li __ f (d) g __ __ ss

Spelling Sums

11. Find list or revision words.

(a) **yes** + **ter** + **day** = _____ (b) **c** + **uff** = _____

(c) **Ap** + **ril** = _____ (d) **M** + **ay** = _____

(e) **st** + **all** = _____ (f) **j** + **azz** = _____

Changing Words

12. Change one letter in each word to make a list or revision word.

(a) grass _____

(b) kiss _____

(c) not _____

(d) skill _____

Additional Activities

13. (a) Write five more words that end in 'ss'. Check your spelling.

(b) Use a dictionary to write a definition for each of your new words.

(c) Write five sentences, each containing one of your new 'ss' words.

Unit 5

Look

Say

Trace

Cover

Write

Check

List Words	Practise	Practise	T	D
bottle				
little				
battle				
rattle				
middle				
riddle				
paddle				
buckle				
ankle				
eagle				
apple				
needle				
able				
rectangle				
single				
jungle				
part				
twelve				

Picture Matching

1. Write the list word that matches each picture.

   (a)

   (b)

   (c) _____

   (d)

What am I?

2. (a) I am an even number.

   I am twice six.

   I am less than thirteen.

   I am _____.

   (b) I can be hard to understand.

   I can be fun.

   I make you think.

   I am a _____.

Unit 5

Crossword

3. Use list words to solve the crossword.

Across
1. A fight or struggle.
4. Something that is hard to understand.
5. You use one to travel in a canoe.
7. To bang, clatter or jangle.
9. A bit or piece.
11. Small.
13. I am ___ to go to the party.
14. It can contain liquid or sauce.
15. A round fruit with red or green skin.
17. The ___ is full of wild animals.
18. You use it for sewing or knitting.

Down
2. It connects a foot to a leg.
3. Central.
6. Only one.
8. A dozen.
10. A shape.
12. A large bird of prey.
16. It's on the end of a belt or strap.

Shape Sorter

4. Write a list word that fits in each shape.

(a)

(b)

(c)

Letters into Words

5. Write six list words using the letters on the hearts.

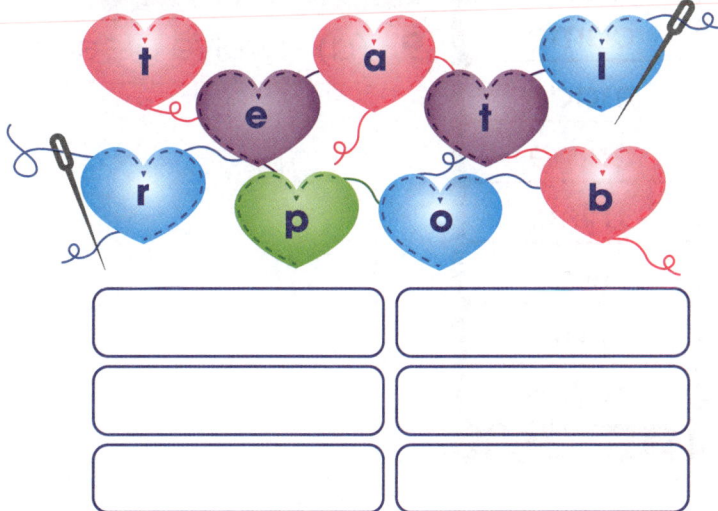

Unit 5

le

List Words

- bottle
- little
- battle
- rattle
- middle
- riddle
- paddle
- buckle
- ankle
- eagle
- apple
- needle
- able
- rectangle
- single
- jungle
- part
- twelve

Revision Words

- make
- came
- made
- crime
- mine
- like
- her
- come

Adding Endings

These words are nouns (naming words). To make them into verbs (doing words), we add 'ing'. When 'ing' is added, 'e' goes away.

6. Add 'ing' to each of these words.

   (a) paddle _____   (b) rattle _____

   (c) battle _____   (d) buckle _____

Missing Words

7. Complete the sentences using list or revision words.

   (a) Dad's belt has a silver _____.

   (b) The _____ lion cub was sad because he was lost in the _____ of the _____.

   (c) I _____ to _____ cakes.

All Mixed Up

8. Unjumble these list and revision words.

   (a) mdledi _____   (b) mreci _____

   (c) tabtel _____   (d) velwet _____

Read and Draw

9. (a) Twelve green bottles   (b) A single red apple

20

Unit 5

Word Search

10. Find the list and revision words in the word search.

bottle	paddle	able
little	buckle	rectangle
battle	ankle	single
rattle	eagle	jungle
middle	apple	part
riddle	needle	twelve
make	came	made
crime	mine	like
her	come	

x	x	m	a	z	t	o	c	m	a	k	e	m
a	k	q	i	v	w	e	r	b	b	t	n	w
m	i	d	d	l	e	r	i	u	a	y	s	p
x	j	u	n	g	l	e	m	c	t	w	i	a
u	h	o	y	l	v	c	e	k	t	b	n	r
n	e	e	d	l	e	t	a	l	l	o	g	t
r	r	s	m	r	l	a	l	e	e	t	l	y
i	c	q	a	a	i	n	i	c	x	t	e	b
d	o	a	d	t	k	g	t	a	d	l	a	a
d	m	b	e	t	e	l	t	m	l	e	g	n
l	e	l	c	l	f	e	l	e	a	n	l	k
e	o	e	t	e	t	l	e	m	i	n	e	l
p	a	d	d	l	e	z	w	a	p	p	l	e

Rhyming Words

11. Choose a rhyming word from your list or revision words.

(a) tingle _____   (b) start _____

(c) same _____   (d) saddle _____

(e) table _____   (f) spike _____

Word Worm

12. Circle each list or revision word you can find in the word worm.

Additional Activities

13. (a) Write four more 'shape' words. Check your spelling.

(b) Write your new shape words in alphabetical order.

(c) For each shape word, write a list of three objects that are usually this shape.

Unit 6

List Words	Practise	Practise	T	D
scrap				
scrape				
scrub				
scream				
screen				
spray				
spread				
sprain				
sprint				
sprout				
stripe				
strap				
straw				
street				
strong				
stream				
live				
usual				

Adding Beginnings

1. Add '**scr**', '**str**', or '**spr**' to make a list word.

   (a) ___ ___ ___ ub

   (b) ___ ___ ___ ay

   (c) ___ ___ ___ ong

   (d) ___ ___ ___ ap

   (e) ___ ___ ___ ape

   (f) ___ ___ ___ ain

Small Words

2. Write the list words that contain these small words.

   (a) us _____

   (b) out _____

   (c) ape _____

   (d) raw _____

   (e) tree _____

   (f) on _____

Unit 6

scr spr str

Crossword

3. Use list words to solve the crossword.

Across

2. To rub against a hard surface.
4. Glass surface of a television.
5. A band or belt.
6. A small, narrow river.
7. To stretch out.
8. Opposite of '**weak**'.
9. Dried stalks of grain.
10. Long strip of a different colour.
11. Normal.

Down

1. To run fast over a short distance.
2. To make a long, loud sound.
3. Tiny drops of liquid moving through the air.
4. A painful wrench of part of the body.
6. Road.
7. To grow or develop.
8. A small piece of something.
10. Rub hard so as to clean.
12. He went to ___ in America.

Spelling Patterns

4. Use the correct colour for these words.

   (a) Colour the 'scr' words **red**.
   (b) Colour the 'spr' words **blue**.
   (c) Colour the 'str' words **green**.

scream   sprout
spray   street
strong   scrap

Unit 6

List Words

- scrap
- scrape
- scrub
- scream
- screen
- spray
- spread
- sprain
- sprint
- sprout
- stripe
- strap
- straw
- street
- strong
- stream
- live
- usual

Revision Words

- woke
- bone
- note
- June
- cube
- use
- seven
- eight

Adding Endings

1. For some words, the endings are just added.
2. For some words, the consonant is doubled to keep the vowel short.
3. 'e' goes away when 'ing' comes to stay.

5. Add the suffixes 's', 'ed' and 'ing' to make new words.

	Add 's'	Add 'ed'	Add 'ing'
(a) live			
(b) use			
(c) spray			
(d) scrub			
(e) sprint			
(f) scrape			

Mixed-up Sentences

6. Unjumble the sentences.

   (a) spray to An can trunk its water. use elephant

   (b) scrub could your hard. scrape hand if you You too

Proofreading

7. Circle the incorrect words and rewrite them correctly in the spaces.

   (a) You can see ate fish in the steam.

   (b) My name and streat were written on the nowt.

Unit 6

Word Search

8. Find the list and revision words in the word search.

scrap	spread	straw
scrape	sprain	street
scrub	sprint	strong
scream	sprout	stream
screen	stripe	live
spray	strap	usual
woke	bone	note
June	cube	use
seven	eight	

l	w	J	c	y	s	c	r	a	p	u	s	e
i	o	u	u	s	p	r	e	a	d	n	p	n
v	k	n	b	s	t	r	e	a	m	o	r	b
e	e	e	e	t	s	p	r	o	u	t	a	f
f	p	s	c	r	e	e	n	y	p	e	y	s
s	s	p	r	i	n	t	u	s	u	a	l	p
c	n	s	x	p	u	s	t	r	a	w	b	r
r	b	t	s	e	m	b	t	k	o	l	d	a
u	f	r	c	x	s	s	t	r	o	n	g	i
b	y	a	r	r	e	a	q	a	m	w	w	n
a	e	p	e	r	v	e	u	e	i	g	h	t
s	c	r	a	p	e	x	b	o	n	e	n	s
r	h	y	m	a	n	s	t	r	e	e	t	x

Secret Words

9. (a) Take 'st' off 'stream' and put in 'c'. _____

    (b) Put 'un' in front of 'usual'. _____

    (c) Add 'een' to the end of 'eight'. _____

    (d) Take 'p' off 'scrap' and put in 'tch'. _____

Word Meanings

10. Draw lines to match the words to their meanings.

(a) sprain — normal

(b) sprint — monitor

(c) screen — twist

(d) usual — dash

Additional Activities

11. (a) Write five more words that start with 'str'. Check your spelling.

    (b) Use a dictionary to write a definition for each of your new 'str' words.

    (c) Write five sentences each containing one of your new 'str' words.

Unit 7 — Christmas

Look

Say

Trace

Cover

Write

Check

List Words	Practise	Practise	T	D
cracker				
lights				
birth				
stocking				
snowflakes				
Advent				
Dasher				
December				
balloon				
greetings				
holiday				
donkey				
Jesus				
Christmas				
Donner				
shopping				
minute				
month				

Letters into Words

1. Write three list words using the letters on the stars. (Letters can be used more than once.)

Missing Letters

2. Complete these list words.

(a) m __ n __ __ e

(b) __ __ v __ __ t

(c) __ __ __ k __ __

(d) h __ __ __ d __ __

(e) __ __ gh __ __

Christmas

Unit 7

Crossword

3. Use list words to solve the crossword.

Across

2. Name of a reindeer who is probably fast.
7. Expression of goodwill.
9. There are 60 of these in an hour.
10. There are 12 of these in a year.
12. The son of God.
15. Blow it up.
16. Pull hard!
17. The ___ calendar was full of sweets.
18. We went on ___ to France.

Down

1. Twelfth month of the year.
3. You only see these when it's cold.
4. On Saturday we went ___ for presents.
5. The Christian festival celebrating Christ's birth.
6. Christmas tree decorations.
8. Mary rode on one.
11. Another of Santa's reindeers.
13. You hope it will be filled.
14. Being born.

Secret Code

a	b	c	d	e	g	h	i	m	n	o	r	s	t	u	x	y	z
1	2	3	4	5	6	7	8	9	10	11	12	13	14	15	16	17	18

4. Use the secret code to find the Christmas message.

___ ___ ___ ___ ___ ___ ___ ___   ___ ___ ___ ___ ___ ___ ___ ___ ___   ___ ___   ___ ___ ___.
(3)(7)(12)(8)(13)(14)(9)(1)(13)   (6)(12)(5)(5)(14)(8)(10)(6)(13)   (14)(11)   (17)(11)(15)

My Spelling Workbook C—Prim-Ed Publishing—www.prim-ed.com

27

Unit 7

Christmas

List Words

- cracker
- lights
- birth
- stocking
- snowflakes
- Advent
- Dasher
- December
- balloon
- greetings
- holiday
- donkey
- Jesus
- Christmas
- Donner
- shopping
- minute
- month

Revision Words

- tinsel
- carrot
- Santa
- carol
- sweets
- sing
- any
- more

Proofreading

5. Circle the incorrect words and rewrite them correctly in the spaces.

(a) Can I shing my favourite karl at the Crismas concert?

(b) Emma fed the doncay a carot.

Missing Words

6. Complete the sentences using one of the list or revision words.

(a) _____ and _____ pull _____'s sleigh.

(b) I hang a _____ on my bed at _____.

(c) Do not blow _____ air into that _____.

(d) We get presents in the _____ of _____.

Word Shapes

7. Write the word that fits in each shape.

(a)

(b)

(c)

(d)

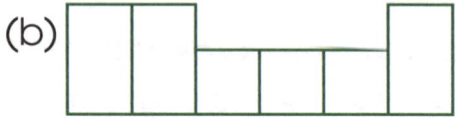

Christmas

Unit 7

Word Search

8. Find the list and revision words in the Christmas tree word search.

- cracker
- birth
- snowflakes
- Dasher
- balloon
- holiday
- Jesus
- Donner
- minute
- tinsel
- Santa
- sweets
- any
- lights
- stocking
- Advent
- December
- greetings
- donkey
- Christmas
- shopping
- month
- carrot
- carol
- sing
- more

Read and Draw

9. Santa is putting gifts under the tree.

What am I?

10. We only last a short time.
We are very, very light.
We sparkle.
We are cold.

We are _____.

Additional Activities

11. (a) Write six more Christmas words. Check your spelling.

(b) Write a Christmas message to your friends.

(c) Write your Christmas list to Santa.

Unit 8

List Words	Practise	Practise	T	D
quit				
quiet				
quite				
liquid				
queen				
question				
quack				
quilt				
quake				
squad				
squash				
squeak				
squirt				
squeal				
squirm				
square				
oil				
during				

Rhyming Words

1. Choose a rhyming word from the list words.

   (a) knit _____
   (b) boil _____
   (c) meal _____
   (d) speak _____
   (e) spare _____
   (f) stack _____

Small Words

2. Find smaller words in these words.

   (a) quite
   (b) square
   (c) during
   (d) question

Unit 8

qu **squ**

Crossword

3. Use list words to solve the crossword.

Across
2. I heard a cat ___ the night.
5. To make a high-pitched scream.
8. To wriggle or twist.
9. A shape with four equal sides.
11. A small number of soldiers.
13. Little or no noise.
15. To shake, especially the earth.
16. A thick cover for a bed.

Down
1. Ask one when you want an answer.
3. To crush until flat.
4. A short high-pitched sound.
6. Water is a ___.
7. Shoot water out from a small hole.
10. My teacher always says '___ right'.
12. The sound made by a duck.
14. Thick greasy liquid.
15. Opposite of king.
16. To leave or stop.

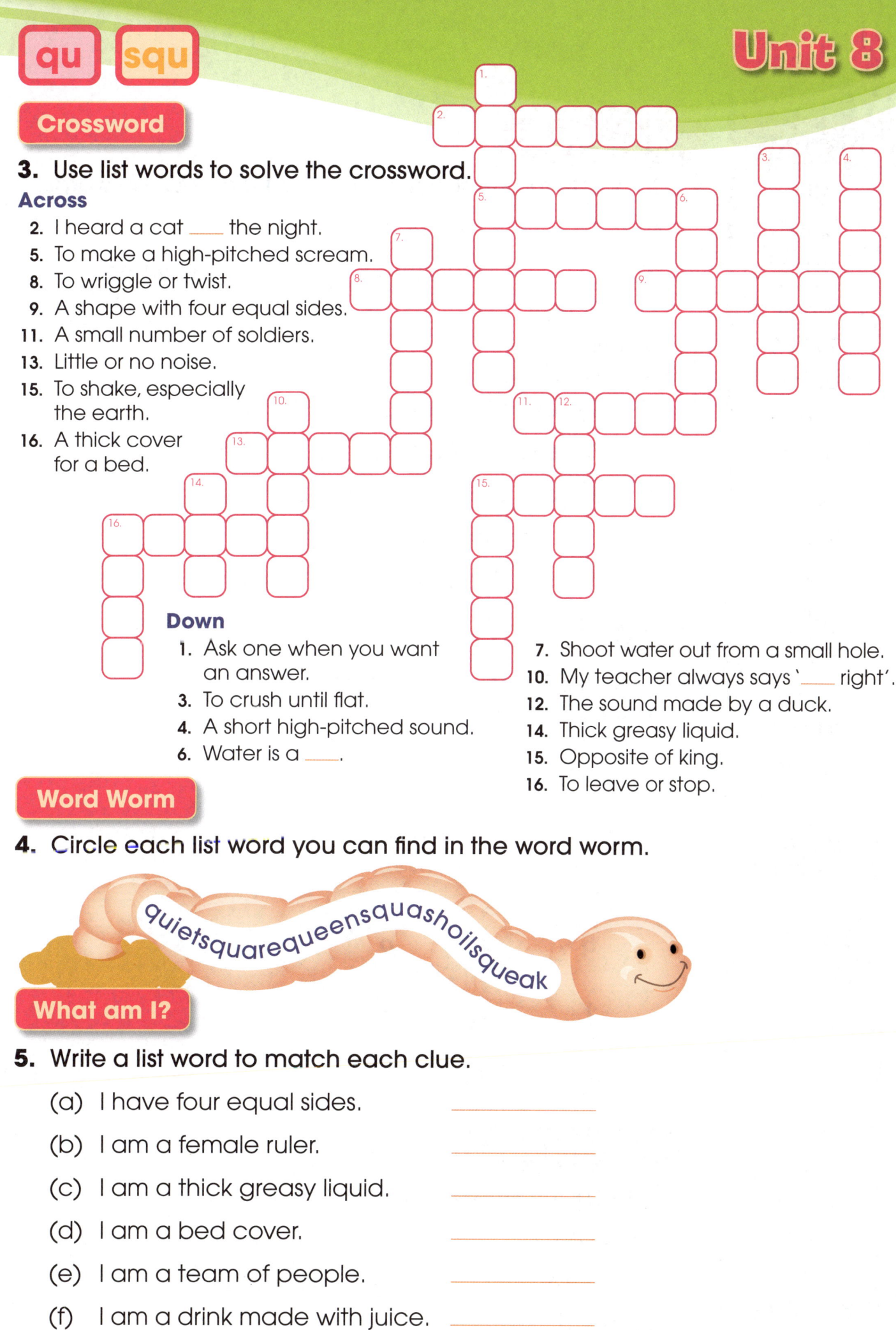

Word Worm

4. Circle each list word you can find in the word worm.

quietsquarequeensquashoilsqueak

What am I?

5. Write a list word to match each clue.

(a) I have four equal sides. _____

(b) I am a female ruler. _____

(c) I am a thick greasy liquid. _____

(d) I am a bed cover. _____

(e) I am a team of people. _____

(f) I am a drink made with juice. _____

Unit 8

List Words

quit
quiet
quite
liquid
queen
question
quack
quilt
quake
squad
squash
squeak
squirt
squeal
squirm
square
oil
during

Missing Words

6. Complete the sentences using the list or revision words.

   (a) _____ the night I heard a mouse _____.

   (b) _____ some _____ on the wheel.

   (c) I always _____ to answer the _____.

Secret Words

7. (a) Take 'qu' off 'quick' and put in 'br'. _____
   (b) Take 'squ' off 'squeal' and put in 'm'. _____
   (c) Take 'a' out of 'quack' and put in 'i'. _____
   (d) Add 'ly' to the end of 'quiet'. _____
   (e) Take 'cr' off 'crash' and put in 'spl'. _____

Letters into Words

8. Write six list or revision words using the letters on the shells.

Revision Words

drop
grab
try
trim
brave
crash
back
give

Change the Tense

9. Change the words to past tense.

   (a) crash _____   (b) question _____
   (c) quack _____   (d) squash _____
   (e) squirt _____   (f) squeak _____

Unit 8

Word Search

10. Find the list and revision words in the word search.

quit	quack	squirt
quiet	quake	squeal
quite	quilt	squirm
liquid	squad	square
queen	squash	oil
question	squeak	during
drop	grab	try
trim	brave	crash
back	give	

q	z	b	r	a	v	e	s	g	s	d	w	f
q	s	q	u	a	d	x	l	i	q	u	i	d
f	s	q	u	a	k	e	b	v	u	r	j	r
b	s	q	u	e	a	l	w	e	i	i	o	o
s	q	u	e	a	k	r	q	y	r	n	k	p
o	i	l	q	u	i	t	u	w	t	g	c	b
q	u	a	c	k	q	x	e	z	j	s	r	x
u	c	r	s	q	u	a	s	h	e	q	a	t
i	q	g	a	y	d	q	t	g	e	u	s	r
t	e	u	t	s	q	u	i	r	m	a	h	y
e	t	r	i	m	k	i	o	x	g	r	a	b
h	q	u	e	e	n	e	n	s	z	e	o	j
c	d	b	a	c	k	t	q	u	i	l	t	z

Antonyms

11. Find list or revision words with the opposite meaning.

(a) take _____   (b) king _____

(c) noisy _____   (d) answer _____

(e) solid _____   (f) front _____

Spelling Patterns

12. Use the correct colour for these words.

(a) Colour the 'qu' words **orange**.

(b) Colour the 'squ' words **green**.

(c) Colour all other words **blue**.

- squad
- quake
- queen
- during
- brave
- squirm

Additional Activities

13. (a) Write five more 'qu' words. Check your spelling.

(b) Use a dictionary to write a definition for each of your new 'qu' words.

(c) Write five sentences, each containing one of your new 'qu' words.

Unit 9

Look

Say

Trace

Cover

Write

Check

List Words	Practise	Practise	T	D
told				
older				
folder				
golden				
scold				
coldest				
boldest				
goldfish				
kindest				
remind				
behind				
find				
mind				
wind				
blind				
grind				
again				
name				

Shape Sorter

1. Write the word that fits in each shape.

   (a)

   (b)

   (c)

   (d)

Changing Words

2. Change one letter in each word to make a list word.

   (a) wand _____

   (b) mine _____

   (c) colder _____

   (d) sold _____

   (e) fond _____

   (f) blend _____

Unit 9

Crossword

3. Use list words to solve the crossword.

Across
1. At the back.
2. Turn a handle to make something work.
4. A pet that swims in a bowl.
6. The most caring.
9. I keep all my papers in a ___.
11. Today was the ___ day of the year.
15. By what someone is known.
16. Coloured like a yellow metal.

Down
1. Put a 'b' in front of oldest.
3. Unable to see.
5. I forgot the answer as my ___ went blank.
7. Past tense of 'tell'.
8. To cause one to remember.
10. Once more.
12. She is six years ___ than I.
13. The teacher had to ___ the naughty boys.
14. To crush coffee beans.

Alphabetical Order

4. Write these words in alphabetical order.

| mind | told | name |
| again | | older |

_____
_____
_____
_____
_____

Word Hunt

5. Which list word …

(a) can be pronounced in two different ways? _____
(b) contains another list word? _____
(c) has the most letters? _____
(d) starts with 'a'? _____

Unit 9

List Words

- told
- older
- folder
- golden
- scold
- coldest
- boldest
- goldfish
- kindest
- remind
- behind
- find
- mind
- wind
- blind
- grind
- again
- name

Revision Words

- start
- stone
- stamp
- nest
- must
- lost
- nine
- help

Comparatives

The suffix 'er' means 'more' and the suffix 'est' means 'most'; for example, tall, taller, tallest.

6. Complete this grid.

Word	'er'	'est'
	older	
cold		
bold		

Secret Code

7. Use the secret code to find the list or revision word.

(a) ___ ___ ___ ___ ___ ___
    (1) (3) (4) (5) (8) (2)

(b) ___ ___ ___ ___
    (8) (5) (8) (3)

(c) ___ ___ ___ ___
    (7) (5) (8) (2)

(d) ___ ___ ___ ___
    (10) (9) (6) (2)

b	1
d	2
e	3
h	4
i	5
l	6
m	7
n	8
o	9
t	10

Read and Draw

8. (a) A goldfish hiding behind a stone

(b) A nest containing a golden egg

Unit 9

Word Search

9. Find the list and revision words in the word search.

told	older	folder
golden	scold	coldest
boldest	goldfish	kindest
remind	behind	find
mind	wind	blind
grind	again	name
start	stone	stamp
nest	must	lost
nine	help	

b	l	i	n	d	d	y	m	b	a	n	j	k
g	r	i	n	d	r	b	u	o	n	s	a	z
t	a	d	u	v	e	j	s	l	s	t	y	n
o	g	v	u	h	m	f	t	d	g	a	h	a
l	a	c	f	u	i	o	b	e	o	r	e	m
d	i	o	g	k	n	l	e	s	l	t	l	e
s	n	l	o	i	d	d	h	t	d	p	p	o
f	i	d	l	n	l	e	i	m	f	a	x	l
j	n	e	d	d	o	r	n	i	i	s	f	d
w	e	s	e	e	s	v	d	n	s	t	x	e
i	t	t	n	s	t	n	c	d	h	o	v	r
n	n	e	s	t	a	m	p	f	i	n	d	i
d	y	n	s	c	o	l	d	d	p	e	r	h

Past Tense

When something has already happened, we often add 'ed' to the word. Some words change altogether:

'**start**' becomes '**started**'

'**bind**' becomes '**bound**'.

10. Change these words to the past tense.

(a) find _____   (b) grind _____

(c) help _____   (d) name _____

Word Worm

11. Circle each list or revision word you can find in the word worm.

Additional Activities

12. (a) Write two adjectives that end in '**old**' and two that end in '**ind**'. Check your spelling.

(b) Add '**er**' to the end of your four new words. Do they make sense?

(c) Add '**est**' to the end of you four new words. Do they make sense?

Unit 10

 Look
 Say
 Trace
 Cover
 Write
 Check

List Words	Practise	Practise	T	D
twice				
price				
spice				
slice				
ice-cream				
rice				
advice				
mice				
voice				
ace				
disgrace				
trace				
space				
place				
race				
face				
January				
because				

Word Building

1. Use the letters in the ice-cream to make 'ice' words.

   _____
   _____
   _____
   _____

-cream, sp, pr, tw, sl

More Word Building

2. Use the letters in the face to make 'ace' words.

   _____
   _____
   _____
   _____
   _____

sp-, pl-, f-, r-, tr-, disgr-

Unit 10

Crossword

3. Use list words to solve the crossword.

Across

2. A playing card with a single symbol.
5. A competition between runners.
7. Two times.
9. A particular position.
12. Cereal grains.
13. Gap.
14. You add this to flavour food.
15. Ideas, help, hints.
17. His bad behaviour was a ___.

Down

1. Mark, sign or evidence.
3. The 1st month.
4. Plural of mouse.
6. He left work ___ he was ill.
8. Soft, frozen, milky dessert.
9. Cost.
10. The part of your head where your nose and eyes are.
11. A piece, portion or wedge.
16. The power of speech.

Word Challenge

4. Make two compound words using the word '**space**'.

Syllables

5. Add the missing syllable to finish the list word.

(a) ice + cream ▶▶▶ _____
(b) dis + ▢ ▶▶▶ _____
(c) be + ▢ ▶▶▶ _____
(d) ad + ▢ ▶▶▶ _____

Unit 10

List Words
- twice
- price
- spice
- slice
- ice-cream
- rice
- advice
- mIce
- voice
- ace
- disgrace
- trace
- space
- place
- race
- face
- January
- because

Revision Words
- skip
- skirt
- spark
- spot
- swim
- sweep
- good
- who

Mixed-up Sentences

6. Unjumble the sentences.

   (a) have I ice-cream? a of cake and slice some May

   _____

   _____

   (b) are best sales. prices in The the January

   _____

   _____

All Mixed Up

7. Unjumble these list and revision words.

   (a) wicet _____   (b) cripe _____

   (c) ebaecus _____   (d) cafe _____

   (e) tops _____   (f) how _____

Secret Words

8. (a) Take 'use' off 'because' and put in 'me'. _____

   (b) Take 'grace' off 'disgrace' and put in 'may'. _____

   (c) Take 'k' off 'spark' and put in 'e'. _____

Read and Draw

9. (a) Three mice in a skipping race

   (b) A sad face with a spot on its chin

Unit 10

Word Search

10. Find the list and revision words in the word search.

twice	advice	space
price	mice	place
spice	voice	race
slice	ace	face
ice-cream	disgrace	January
rice	trace	because
skip	skirt	spark
spot	swim	sweep
good	who	

y	e	p	r	i	c	e	k	b	p	q	b	i
y	s	a	p	d	i	s	g	r	a	c	e	c
s	l	w	c	s	p	a	r	k	s	m	c	e
k	i	u	t	r	i	q	i	e	k	z	a	c
i	c	z	w	f	f	s	c	t	i	n	u	r
p	e	g	i	r	a	c	e	r	r	g	s	e
s	p	a	c	e	w	l	g	a	t	p	e	a
u	s	w	e	e	p	m	i	c	e	l	j	m
s	g	s	w	i	m	a	c	e	i	a	h	w
p	o	e	m	c	u	a	d	v	i	c	e	f
o	o	t	o	a	s	p	i	c	e	e	n	a
t	d	J	a	n	u	a	r	y	a	x	f	c
w	h	o	p	l	y	v	o	i	c	e	b	e

Spelling Sums

11. Find list or revision words.

(a) **be + cause** = ☐

(b) **sw + eep** = ☐

(c) **tr + ace** = ☐

(d) **pl + ace** = ☐

(e) **m + ice** = ☐

(f) **sp + ark** = ☐

Spelling Patterns

12. Use the correct colour for these words.

(a) Colour the 'ace' words **yellow**.

(b) Colour the 'ice' words **blue**.

(c) Colour the other words **red**.

who	voice
disgrace	advice
trace	January

Additional Activities

13. (a) Write two more 'ace' words and two more 'ice' words. Check your spelling.

(b) Use a dictionary to write a definition for each of your new 'ace' and 'ice' words.

(c) Write four sentences, each containing one of your new 'ace' and 'ice' words.

Unit 11

List Words	Practise	Practise	T	D
page				
huge				
stage				
cage				
bandage				
bridge				
badge				
hedge				
judge				
bench				
branch				
crunch				
wrench				
match				
watch				
catch				
please				
February				

Missing Letters

1. Add '**ge**' or '**dge**' to make list words.

    (a) bri _____

    (b) hu _____

    (c) pa _____

    (d) ba _____

    (e) he _____

    (f) banda _____

More Missing Letters

2. Add '**ch**' or '**tch**' to make list words.

    (a) ben _____

    (b) ca _____

    (c) wa _____

    (d) crun _____

    (e) wren _____

    (f) bran _____

Unit 11

Crossword

3. Use list words to solve the crossword.

Across
4. Bushes that can make a fence.
5. A sudden twist or pull.
8. A packet of crisps, ___.
11. Material for a wound.
12. My mum's shoes and bag always ___.
14. The leaf of a book.
15. He had to ___ the singing competition.
16. Vast, gigantic or enormous.

Down
1. It can be built over a river.
2. The parrot often came out of its ___.
3. A long seat.
5. It tells you the time.
6. To crush with the teeth.
7. Part of a tree.
9. Actors perform on a ___.
10. The shortest month of the year.
11. We have a ___ on our blazer.
13. To take hold or seize.

Plurals

4. Add 's' or 'es' to make the list words plural.

(a) page _____
(b) match _____
(c) badge _____
(d) branch _____
(e) bridge _____
(f) bandage _____

Alphabetical Order

5. Write these words in alphabetical order.

| huge | cage | watch |
| stage | | bench |

_____
_____
_____
_____
_____
_____

My Spelling Workbook C—Prim-Ed Publishing—www.prim-ed.com

Unit 11

List Words

- page
- huge
- stage
- cage
- bandage
- bridge
- badge
- hedge
- judge
- bench
- branch
- crunch
- wrench
- match
- watch
- catch
- please
- February

Revision Words

- spent
- rent
- went
- grant
- camp
- bump
- some
- their

Compound Words

6. Write a list or revision word that can be added to make a compound word.

(a) _____ dog   (b) _____ site

(c) _____ mark   (d) bird _____

(e) _____ where   (f) _____ phrase

Small Words

7. Find small words in these list or revision words.

(a) branch [   ] [   ]

            [   ] [   ]

(b) hedge   [   ]

(c) badge   [   ]

(d) bridge [   ] [   ]

(e) crunch [   ]

(f) match   [   ] [   ]

Synonyms

8. Find a list or revision word with a similar meaning.

(a) enormous _____   (b) hire _____

(c) referee _____   (d) knock _____

(e) spanner _____   (f) allow _____

Two Meanings

9. The word '**watch**' has two meanings. One has been drawn. Draw another meaning.

Unit 11

Word Search

10. Find the list and revision words in the word search.

page	badge	wrench
huge	hedge	match
stage	judge	watch
cage	bench	catch
bandage	branch	please
bridge	crunch	February
spent	went	rent
grant	camp	bump
some	their	

o	w	a	t	c	h	q	s	p	e	n	t	r
a	b	u	m	p	u	r	i	j	u	d	g	e
k	b	r	a	n	c	h	p	a	g	e	x	n
w	m	a	t	c	h	e	d	g	e	d	f	t
y	d	b	a	n	d	a	g	e	l	i	s	c
e	d	e	F	e	b	r	u	a	r	y	a	a
s	j	n	r	w	e	n	t	i	b	h	w	m
t	y	c	z	x	c	a	g	e	a	r	r	p
a	t	h	e	i	r	b	r	i	d	g	e	f
g	x	z	r	s	h	u	g	e	g	c	n	w
e	p	c	a	t	c	h	o	o	e	v	c	x
p	l	e	a	s	e	g	r	a	n	t	h	e
s	o	m	e	d	c	r	u	n	c	h	m	f

Missing Words

11. Complete the sentences using these list or revision words.

| bench   watch   huge   please   February   match   spent   their |

(a) The children were crying because _____ bikes had been stolen.

(b) May I have a biscuit, _____?

(c) We will sit on the _____ and _____ the _____.

(d) There are 28 days in _____ and 29 days in a leap year.

(e) I _____ all my money on a _____ ice-cream.

Additional Activities

12. (a) Write six more months of the year. Check your spelling.

(b) Write your new month words in alphabetical order.

(c) For each month word, write an event that usually occurs during that month.

Unit 12

Compound Words

Look

Say

Trace

Cover

Write

Check

List Words	Practise	Practise	T	D
yourself				
himself				
herself				
myself				
outside				
inside				
offside				
seaside				
someone				
something				
sometimes				
somebody				
everyone				
everything				
everybody				
everywhere				
centimetre				
metre				

Compound Words

1. Draw lines to make compound words.

   (a) every • • side
   (b) sea • • times
   (c) him • • body
   (d) some • • self

Letters into Words

2. Write three list words using the letters in the hearts. (Letters can be used more than once.)

Hearts: s, e, i, a, d, c, n, r, o, f, t

Compound Words

Unit 12

Crossword

3. Use list words to solve the crossword.

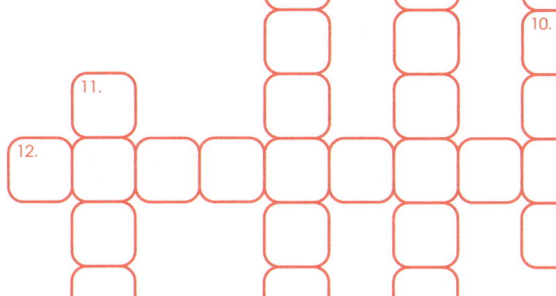

Across
1. Someone.
6. Somebody.
7. 100 centimetres.
10. You.
12. All things.
14. Interior.
17. Now and then.
18. Opposite of 'himself'.

Down
2. Opposite of 'inside'.
3. Every person.
4. A metric unit of length.
5. An unknown thing.
8. All the people.
9. The football player was ____.
11. In all places.
13. Opposite of 'herself'.
15. Me.
16. A beach area.

Small Words

4. Write the list words that contain these small words.

(a) as _____

(b) our _____

(c) cent _____

(d) of _____

(e) here _____

Unit 12

Compound Words

List Words

- yourself
- himself
- herself
- myself
- outside
- inside
- offside
- seaside
- someone
- something
- sometimes
- somebody
- everyone
- everything
- everybody
- everywhere
- centimetre
- metre

Revision Words

- meat
- teach
- dear
- hear
- keep
- sleep
- would
- pupil

Word Hunt

5. (a) Which list words have a 'th' sound?

_____ _____

(b) Which revision word is part of an eye? _____

(c) Which list word is used in football? _____

(d) Which list and revision words contain a double letter?

_____ _____ _____

All Mixed Up

6. Unjumble these list and revision words.

(a) siiden _____   (b) dare _____

(c) uroslyfe _____   (d) olwud _____

(e) esiased _____   (f) terem _____

Missing Words

7. Complete the sentences using list or revision words.

(a) _____ I'm allowed to stay up late.

(b) Can you _____ me to skate?

(c) Come _____ out of the rain.

(d) Put the baby to bed for a _____.

Read and Draw

8. (a) Yourself at the seaside

(b) Someone eating a meat pie

Compound Words — Unit 12

Word Search

9. Find the list and revision words in the word search.

yourself	offside
everyone	himself
seaside	everything
herself	someone
everybody	myself
something	everywhere
outside	sometimes
centimetre	inside
somebody	metre
meat	teach
dear	hear
keep	sleep
would	pupil

```
u f e s o m e b o d y p r l t
e s o m e t i m e s l m o r w
w e v e r y w h e r e e t h e
q e v e r y t h i n g t u i v
b e h e r s e l f i a r e m e
s m e p o w o u l d v e d s r
o e p u p i l s e a s i d e y
m a o g y i n s i d e h k l o
e t x a m y s e l f o e e f n
t s o u t s i d e t b a e i e
h e y o u r s e l f r r p t s
i o d b e v e r y b o d y e l
n c e n t i m e t r e f n a e
g p a s o m e o n e g d w c e
f i r s o f f s i d e r l h p
```

Shape Sorter

10. Write the word that fits in each shape.

(a) ⬚⬚⬚⬚⬚⬚⬚ (b) ⬚⬚⬚⬚⬚⬚⬚⬚⬚ (c) ⬚⬚⬚⬚⬚⬚

Word Worm

11. Circle each list or revision word you can find in the word worm.

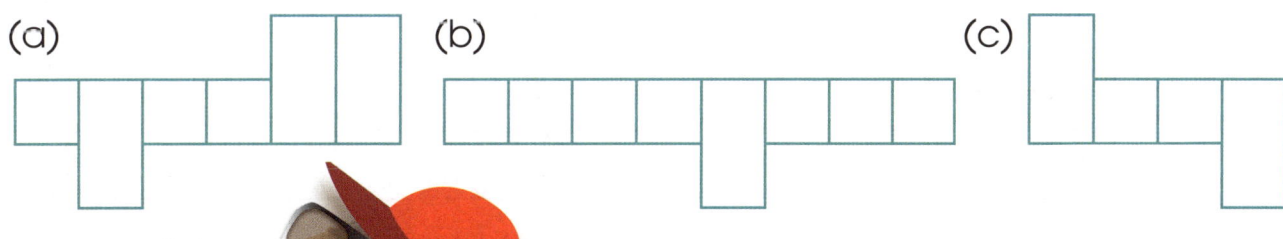

Additional Activities

12. (a) Write five more compound words. Check your spelling.

(b) Write your five new compound words in alphabetical order.

(c) Write five sentences each containing one of your new compound words.

Unit 13

Spring/Easter

Look

Say

Trace

Cover

Write

Check

List Words	Practise	Practise	T	D
Easter				
bonnet				
cloud				
crocus				
grass				
green				
fresh				
buttercup				
butterfly				
digging				
dragonfly				
Christ				
bluebird				
pray				
death				
ladybird				
eighteen				
seventeen				

Small Words

1. Write the list word that contains these small words.

   (a) on _____ _____
   (b) at _____
   (c) us _____
   (d) is _____
   (e) as _____ _____

All Mixed Up

2. Unjumble these list words.

   (a) hrfes _____
   (b) ryap _____
   (c) oclud _____
   (d) rladidby _____
   (e) nevetenes _____
   (f) berlidub _____

Spring/Easter

Unit 13

Crossword

3. Use list words to solve the crossword.

Across
2. Small songbird.
5. The opposite of 'birth'.
7. At church, we ___ together.
9. Yellow flower.
11. The fruit is ___, not tinned.
12. Can bring rain.
13. Similar to a moth.
15. He had a spade and was ___ in the garden.
17. Three less than twenty.

Down
1. The colour of grass.
2. A head covering.
3. Has long lacy wings.
4. Red with black dots.
6. The name for Jesus.
8. Time when Christians celebrate the rising of Christ.
10. Small flower.
14. Two greater than sixteen.
16. Lawn.

Secret Words

4. (a) Take 'Ea' off 'Easter' and put in 'ham'. _____

(b) Take 'bird' off 'bluebird' and put in 'bell'. _____

(c) Take 'teen' off 'seventeen' and put in 'th'. _____

(d) Take 'cl' off 'cloud' and put in 'pr'. _____

Unit 13 — Spring/Easter

List Words
- Easter
- bonnet
- cloud
- crocus
- grass
- green
- fresh
- buttercup
- butterfly
- digging
- dragonfly
- Christ
- bluebird
- pray
- death
- ladybird
- eighteen
- seventeen

Revision Words
- flower
- bunny
- basket
- warm
- raindrop
- spring
- thirteen
- Monday

Compound Words

5. Match the words to make compound words.

(a) dragon — drop
(b) butter — bird
(c) rain — fly
(d) blue — cup

Mixed-up Sentences

6. Unjumble these sentences and write them correctly.

(a) on ladybird crocus. The sipped the raindrop the
_____

(b) Monday bonnets. we On thirteen made Easter
_____

Changing Words

7. Change one letter in each word to make a list or revision word.

(a) warp _____   (b) casket _____
(c) glass _____   (d) flesh _____

Word Worm

8. Circle each list or revision word you can find in the word worm.

diggingprayMondayfreshbonnetEaster

Unit 13

Spring/Easter

Word Search

9. Find the list and revision words in the Easter egg word search.

Easter
cloud
grass
fresh
butterfly
digging
dragonfly
Christ
bluebird
pray
death
ladybird
eighteen
bunny
warm
spring
Monday

bonnet
crocus
green
buttercup

seventeen
flower
basket
raindrop
thirteen

Word Hunt

10. (a) Which three words are insects?

    (b) Which three words are numbers?

    (c) Which word rhymes with 'focus'?

Additional Activities

11. (a) Write six more Easter or spring words. Check your spelling.

    (b) Write an Easter message.

    (c) Find and write six more compound words.

Unit 14

Contractions

List Words	Practise	Practise	T	D
weren't				
I'd				
won't				
we've				
they've				
what's				
that's				
there's				
you're				
hasn't				
you've				
we're				
she's				
you'll				
they'd				
they're				
Wales				
Scotland				

Word Hunt

1. Which list word(s)

   (a) begins with 'h'?

   (b) have the letters 've'?

   (c) have the contraction of the word 'not' in them?

   (d) are countries?

   (e) has the smallest number of letters?

Contractions

Unit 14

Crossword

2. Use list words to solve the crossword.

Across

2. Short for has not.
3. Short for we are.
5. Short for she is.
6. Short for that is.
10. Short for there is.
11. Short for you will or shall.
12. Short for you have.
14. Short for they are.
15. Short for they had or would.

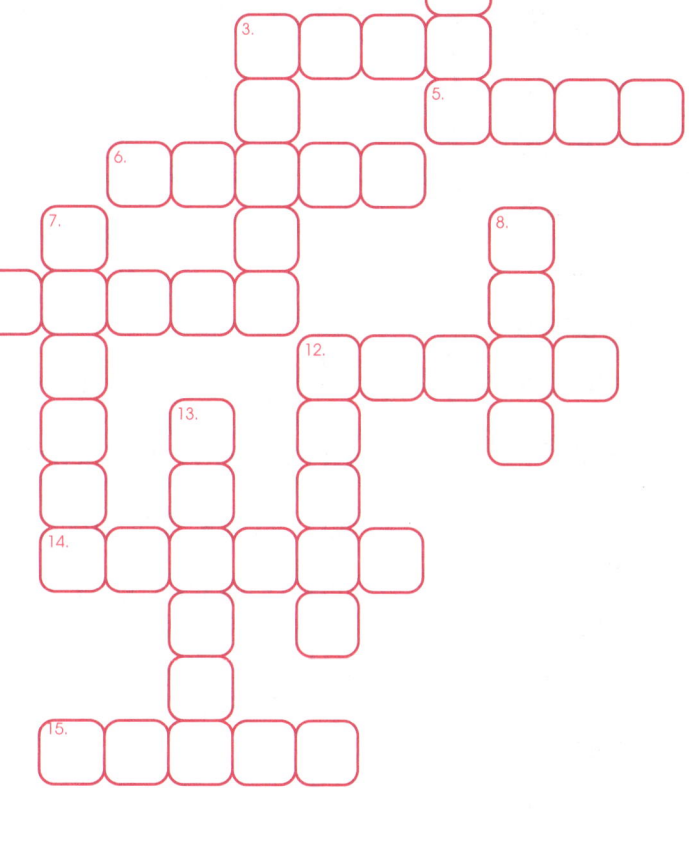

Down

1. Cardiff is its capital city.
3. Short for what is.
4. Edinburgh is its capital city.
7. Short for were not.
8. Short for we have
9. Short for will not.
12. Short for you are.
13. Short for they have.

Changing Words

3. Change one letter in each word to make a list word.

(a) they've _____

(b) she'd _____

(c) you're _____

(d) walks _____

Letters into Words

4. Write four list words using the letters in the stars. (Letters can be used more than once.)

Letters: r, v, ', y, h, t, e, s, d

Unit 14 — Contractions

List Words
weren't, I'd, won't, we've, they've, what's, that's, there's, you're, hasn't, you've, we're, she's, you'll, they'd, they're, Wales, Scotland

Revision Words
bang, along, belong, thing, being, hung, old, has

Contractions

5. Write the contractions.

(a) you will _____   (b) she is _____
(c) what is _____   (d) I had _____
(e) they are _____   (f) will not _____
(g) we are _____   (h) there is _____

Missing Words

6. Complete the sentences using list or revision words.

(a) Walk carefully _____ the wall.

(b) Susan is sick, so _____ not been at school.

(c) My friends are happy, as _____ all going to the circus.

(d) _____ not fair, I didn't break the window!

Alphabetical Order

7. Write these list and revision words in alphabetical order.

> you're   Scotland
> what's   that's
> old

_____
_____
_____
_____
_____

All Mixed Up

8. Unjumble these list and revision words. Use a coloured pencil to place the apostrophe in the words.

(a) uyero _____
(b) gunh _____
(c) veew _____
(d) hatts _____
(e) deyht _____
(f) legonb _____

Contractions

Unit 14

Word Search

9. Find the list and revision words in the word search.

weren't	that's	she's
I'd	there's	they'd
won't	you're	Wales
we've	hasn't	Scotland
they've	you've	belong
what's	we're	hung
bang	along	has
thing	being	old
you'll	they're	

t	h	e	y	've	y	o	h	u	n	g	n
h	l	k	o	m	w	e	r	e	n	't	w
i	y	o	u	're	t	a	S	s	h	e	's
n	s	b	'l	a	i	h	P	c	t	S	c	o
g	h	e	l	l	t	e	w	o	n	't	s	t
d	e	i	b	o	h	y	p	t	o	l	d	h
l	'd	n	a	n	a	'r	s	l	r	e	n	e
w	t	g	a	g	t	e	h	a	s	n	't	y
e	h	h	l	w	's	b	a	n	g	c	o	'd
'v	W	a	l	e	s	W	a	d	s	l	a	n
e	o	s	g	'r	p	f	v	w	h	a	t	's
c	g	h	b	e	l	o	n	g	v	e	u	w
y	o	u	've	g	b	t	h	e	r	e	's

Shape Sorter

10. Write a list or revision word that fits in each shape.

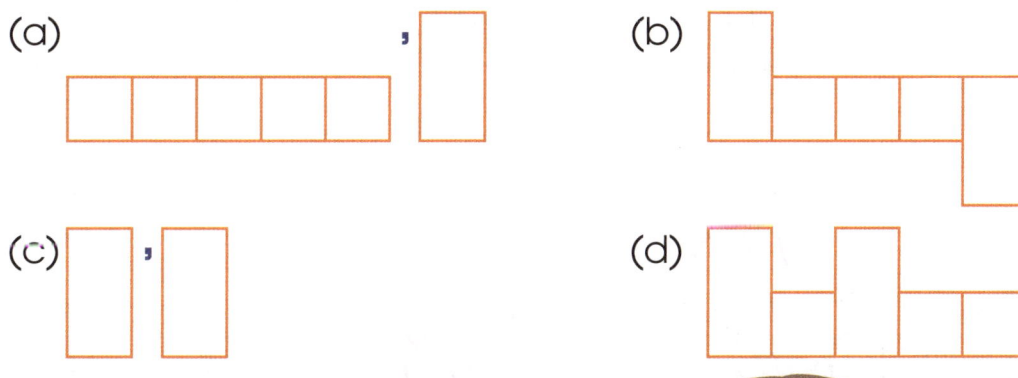

Word Worm

11. Circle each list or revision word you can find in the word worm.

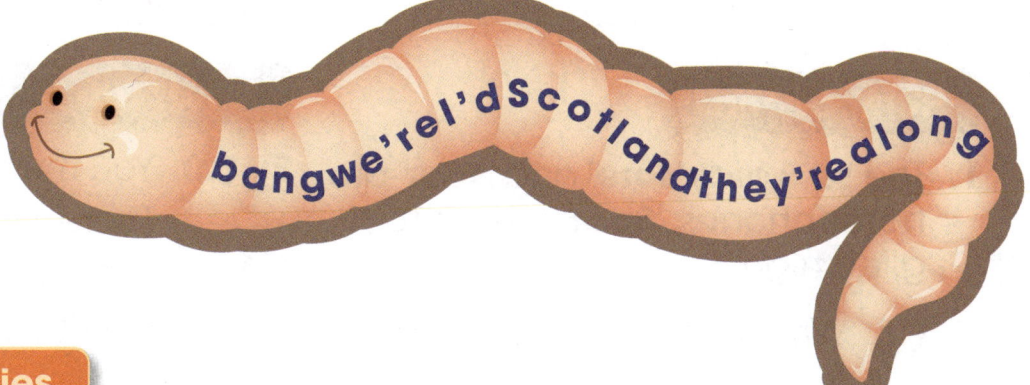

Additional Activities

12. (a) Write three more contractions. Check your spelling.

(b) Write your three new contractions in their full form; e.g. 'they've' — 'they have'.

(c) Write three sentences, each containing one of your new words.

Unit 15

 Look
 Say
 Trace
 Cover
 Write
 Check

List Words	Practise	Practise	T	D
draw	draw	draw		
straw	straw	straw		
law	law			
claw	claw			
soar	soar			
board	board			
oar	oar			
roar	roar			
sore	sore			
tore	tore			
more	more			
score	score			
stalk	stalk			
walk	walk			
talk	talk			
chalk	chalk			
today	today	today		
year	year	year		

Homophones

1. The list words '**sore**' and '**soar**' are homophones. '**Soar**' means to glide high.

    (a) Write a definition for '**sore**'.

    _____

    (b) Write a sentence using '**sore**'.

    _____

What am I?

2. (a) You must obey me.
    There are different kinds.
    There is a price to pay if you break me.

    I am the _____.

    (b) I am usually long and thin.
    I am sometimes coloured.
    I am used for writing or drawing.

    I am _____.

Unit 15

Crossword

3. Use list words to solve the crossword.

Across
2. Extra
3. Curved nail of an animal.
4. The rules of a country.
7. Use the power of speech.
9. Long, thin, flat piece of wood.
10. She ___ open the present.
12. Number of goals.
13. 365 days.
14. Fly high into the air.

Down
1. Make a picture.
3. Use it to write on a blackboard.
5. Go on foot.
6. Painful or aching.
7. The day after yesterday.
8. The ___ of a lion is very loud.
11. You use it to row a boat.
12. A thin, hollow tube used for drinking.
14. The stem of a plant.

Spelling Patterns

4. Use the correct colour for these words.

(a) Colour the 'aw' words **red**.
(b) Colour the 'oar' words **blue**.
(c) Colour the 'ore' words **green**.

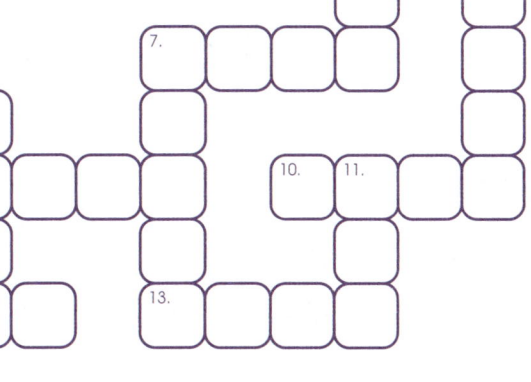

board · score · claw · roar · more · year

Unit 15

aw oar ore a

List Words

- draw
- straw
- law
- claw
- soar
- board
- oar
- roar
- sore
- tore
- more
- score
- stalk
- walk
- talk
- chalk
- today
- year

Revision Words

- away
- day
- stay
- tail
- wait
- train
- Tuesday
- Wednesday

All Mixed Up

5. Unjumble these list and revision words.

   (a) eary _____   (b) kalt _____
   (c) taswr _____   (d) emor _____
   (e) oecsr _____   (f) ritan _____
   (g) tiwa _____   (h) skalt _____

Suffixes

6. Add the suffixes 'ed', 'ing' or 'er' to make new words.

	'ed'	'ing'	'er'
walk	walked	walking	
board	boarded	boarding	
talk	talked	talking	
wait	waited	waiting	

Compound Words

7. Write a list or revision word to make these compound words.

   (a) _____ light   (b) _____ berry
   (c) _____ back   (d) over _____
   (e) _____ way   (f) _____ bridge

Missing Words

8. Complete the sentences using list or revision words.

   (a) Watch the plane _____ into the sky.
   (b) Who do you think will _score_ the first goal?
   (c) _____ here until the _____ has moved down the track.
   (d) Please may I have some _____ milk?

Unit 15

Word Search

9. Find the list and revision words in the word search.

draw	oar	stalk
straw	roar	walk
law	sore	talk
claw	tore	chalk
soar	more	today
board	score	year
away	day	stay
tail	wait	train
Tuesday	Wednesday	

s	j	t	w	a	l	k	z	f	l	u	z	s
c	b	o	a	r	d	t	m	p	a	m	t	t
o	q	r	t	c	l	a	w	n	j	o	a	a
r	h	e	T	v	a	m	c	v	t	r	l	l
e	g	o	u	w	w	q	h	r	r	e	k	k
c	q	a	e	o	d	t	a	m	a	o	t	s
g	k	r	s	c	r	a	l	s	i	n	w	o
s	r	a	d	r	a	i	k	t	n	o	y	r
t	o	d	a	y	w	l	i	s	o	a	r	e
a	r	i	y	a	w	a	y	s	y	e	a	r
y	o	q	x	a	d	a	y	r	l	q	g	f
w	a	i	t	l	m	s	t	r	a	w	b	y
m	r	W	e	d	n	e	s	d	a	y	y	m

Missing Letters

10. Add the correct letters to complete the list or revision words.

(a) dr aw   (b) st a lk
(c) t ai l   (d) oa r
(e) to day   (f) Wed nes day
(g) t a lk   (h) w ai t

Word Meanings

11. Draw lines to match the words to their meanings.

Additional Activities

12. (a) 'Today' and 'year' are time words. Write four more time words. Check your spelling.

(b) Use a dictionary to write a definition for each of your new time words.

(c) Write four sentences, each containing one of your new time words.

Unit 16

List Words	Practise	Practise	T	D
war				
warrior				
warp				
warning				
ward				
wardrobe				
warn				
warmth				
swarm				
dwarf				
award				
warden				
towards				
warren				
reward				
warlock				
fortnight				
second				

Small Words

1. Write the list words that contain these small words.

   (a) or _____ _____

   (b) arm _____ _____

   (c) rob _____

   (d) on _____

   (e) den _____

   (f) in _____

What am I?

2. (a) I am a man.
   I often wear unusual clothes.
   I cast spells.
   I am a _____.

   (b) I am brave.
   I fight with the enemy.
   I carry weapons.
   I am a _____.

Unit 16

Crossword

3. Use list words to solve the crossword.

Across
1. Rabbits live here underground.
3. A fighting man.
4. A male witch.
6. Two weeks.
8. To advise, urge or inform.
9. She was in ___ 7 at the hospital.
10. There was a storm ___ before the storm.
11. After the first.
13. A group of bees and their queen.
15. To become twisted or out of shape.

Down
2. He got a ___ for finding the wallet.
3. A tall cupboard for hanging clothes.
5. A traffic ___.
7. In the direction of.
10. Heat.
12. Happy or Grumpy or Doc.
14. A prize or trophy.
15. How long did the 2nd World ___ last?

Compound Words

4. Draw lines to make compound words.

(a) fort • • lock
(b) ward • • night
(c) war • • robe

Letters into Words

5. Write six list words using the letters in the stars. (Letters can be used more than once.)

Stars: a, w, d, n, r, p, f

Unit 16

List Words

- war
- warrior
- warp
- warning
- ward
- wardrobe
- warn
- warmth
- swarm
- dwarf
- award
- warden
- towards
- warren
- reward
- warlock
- fortnight
- second

Revision Words

- girl
- first
- hurt
- turn
- never
- over
- Thursday
- Friday

Mixed-up Sentences

6. Unjumble the sentences.

    (a) before. girl of never seen had a swarm The bees

    _____

    (b) was an time fortnight. given a for He award second in the

    _____

Antonyms

7. Write a list or revision word with the opposite meaning.

    (a) punishment ☐   (b) giant ☐
    (c) coolness ☐   (d) often ☐
    (e) peace ☐   (f) boy ☐

Missing Letters

8. Add the correct letters to complete the list or revision words.

    (a) __ h __ r __ __ ay   (b) f __ __ __ n __ __ __ t
    (c) __ e __ er   (d) s __ c __ __ d

Read and Draw

9. (a) A warlock casting a spell

   (b) A swarm of bees chasing a dwarf

Unit 16

war

Word Search

10. Find the list and revision words in the word search.

war	warn	towards
warrior	warmth	warren
warp	swarm	reward
warning	dwarf	warlock
ward	award	fortnight
wardrobe	warden	second
girl	first	hurt
turn	never	over
Thursday	Friday	

a	w	a	r	d	e	n	i	f	w	a	r	d
w	p	w	f	o	r	t	n	i	g	h	t	F
a	w	a	r	r	e	n	n	e	v	e	r	r
r	p	t	f	i	r	s	t	w	a	r	n	i
d	r	o	w	w	a	r	p	w	t	t	v	d
w	e	w	a	d	y	s	w	a	r	m	p	a
w	w	a	r	w	T	h	u	r	s	d	a	y
a	a	r	r	a	v	h	x	d	g	i	r	l
r	r	d	i	r	x	a	y	r	q	p	u	y
n	d	s	o	f	j	f	b	o	h	u	r	t
i	w	a	r	l	o	c	k	b	t	u	r	n
n	k	o	v	e	r	o	s	e	c	o	n	d
g	w	a	r	w	a	r	m	t	h	s	n	

Spelling Sums

11. Find list or revision words.

(a) **ward + robe** = _____

(b) **Fri + day** = _____

(c) **re + ward** = _____

(d) **war + rior** = _____

(e) **fir + st** = _____

(f) **warm + th** = _____

Synonyms

12. Find a list or revision word with a similar meaning.

(a) fighter
(b) twist
(c) harm
(d) burrow
(e) prize

Additional Activities

13. (a) 'Second' is an ordinal number. Use a dictionary to write a definition of an ordinal number.

(b) Write four more ordinal numbers. Check your spelling.

(c) Write four sentences, each containing one of your new ordinal number words.

Unit 17

Silent Letters

Look

Say

Trace

Cover

Write

Check

List Words	Practise	Practise	T	D
comb				
lamb				
limb				
numb				
crumb				
wrap				
wreck				
write				
wrong				
honest				
ghost				
hour				
know				
knight				
knife				
knot				
tomorrow				
England				

Silent Letters

1. Sort the list words into family groups.

(a) Silent 'b'

(b) Silent 'w'

(c) Silent 'h'

(d) Silent 'k'

Silent Letters

Unit 17

Crossword

2. Use list words to solve the crossword.

Across

2. To cover something.
4. It cuts.
6. The day after today.
10. It was so cold my toes were ___!
12. Opposite of 'right'.
13. Make a ___ in your tie.
14. A young sheep.
15. I ___ how to swim.
17. It rhymes with 'toast'.
18. An arm or leg of a person.

Down

1. Mark something down on paper.
3. He was a ___ in shining armour.
5. A very small bit of biscuit or bread.
7. The divers found a ship ___.
8. 60 minutes.
9. London is its capital city.
11. Truthful.
16. A brush and ___.

What am I?

3. (a) I am less than a day.
I am more than a second.
There are 60 minutes in me.
I am an _____.

(b) I have teeth.
I am used daily.
I help to make you look tidy.
I am a _____.

Unit 17

Silent Letters

List Words
- comb
- lamb
- limb
- numb
- crumb
- wrap
- wreck
- write
- wrong
- honest
- ghost
- hour
- know
- knight
- knife
- knot
- tomorrow
- England

Revision Words
- loaf
- float
- soap
- below
- own
- crow
- Saturday
- Sunday

Proofreading

4. A list or revision word has been incorrectly spelt in each sentence. Circle it and write it correctly on the line.

(a) There was not a crum left on the plate.

(b) I am going to a football match on Saterday.

(c) Rap your lunch in cling film.

(d) If you're honist you tell the truth.

(e) Wash your hands with sope and water.

(f) I no the answer to that question.

Word Hunt

5. Which list or revision word(s):

(a) has London as its capital city?

(b) has the least letters?

(c) are at the weekend?

(d) means 'legs or arms'?

(e) is a spirit?

Changing Words

6. Change one letter in each word to make a list or revision word.

(a) trap _____   (b) soup _____

(c) bomb _____   (d) lame _____

(e) owe _____   (f) wring _____

(g) grow _____   (h) pour _____

Unit 17

Silent Letters

Word Search

7. Find the list and revision words in the word search.

comb	wreck	know
lamb	write	knight
limb	wrong	knife
numb	honest	knot
crumb	ghost	tomorrow
wrap	hour	England
loaf	float	soap
below	own	crow
Saturday	Sunday	

t	f	j	S	a	t	u	r	d	a	y	l	u
k	l	k	f	d	y	c	r	u	m	b	i	c
h	o	n	e	s	t	y	e	r	l	a	m	b
z	a	i	l	h	n	i	l	o	a	f	b	p
w	t	f	s	c	k	b	t	z	w	r	n	t
r	S	e	g	o	n	e	o	l	r	E	u	c
e	u	s	h	m	o	l	m	b	i	n	m	r
c	n	t	o	b	w	o	o	m	t	g	b	o
k	d	o	s	o	o	w	r	f	e	l	v	w
n	a	w	t	f	w	i	r	s	o	a	p	k
a	y	n	t	a	w	r	o	n	g	n	x	n
t	w	r	a	p	e	p	w	p	u	d	l	o
k	n	i	g	h	t	h	o	u	r	c	o	t

Rhyming Words

8. Choose a rhyming word from the list or revision words.

(a) boat _____   (b) roast _____

(c) strap _____   (d) song _____

(e) life _____   (f) bone _____

Homophones

Homophones are words that are pronounced the same but have a different meaning and spelling.

9. Can you find the homophone to match these words?

(a) night _____

(b) not _____

(c) right _____

(d) no _____

Additional Activities

10. (a) 'England' is the name of a country. Write five more country names. Check your spelling.

(b) Write the capital city of each of your new countries in a sentence; e.g. 'London is the capital city of England'.

Unit 18

Summer Holidays

Look

Say

Trace

Cover

Write

Check

List Words	Practise	Practise	T	D
plane				
atlas				
boat				
crab				
passport				
rock				
flipflops				
beach				
flight				
ticket				
runway				
landing				
pool				
hotel				
salty				
uniform				
said				
there				

Secret Words

1. (a) Change 'pass' to 're' in 'passport'. _____
   (b) Change 'run' to 'high' in 'runway'. _____
   (c) Take 'b' from 'beach' and put in 't'. _____
   (d) Change 'uni' to 'per' in 'uniform'. _____

Synonyms

2. Find list words with similar meanings.

   (a) identification _____   (b) pond _____
   (c) ship _____   (d) airstrip _____
   (e) seashore _____   (f) boulder _____

Summer Holidays

Unit 18

Crossword

3. Use list words to solve the crossword.

Across

3. The teacher ___, 'Be quiet'.
6. Has a hard shell.
7. A hard mineral material of the earth's crust.
8. Landing strip.
9. Footwear.
12. Book me a room at the ___.
14. It floats.
15. You need this when you travel abroad.

Down

1. A soldier's clothing.
2. A book of maps.
3. You cannot drink sea water as it is ___.
4. Needed to get on a plane.
5. The plane will be ___ at 3 o'clock.
10. A journey made in an aircraft.
11. 'Aero___'.
13. In or at that place.
14. Seaside.
16. A pond; puddle.

Secret Code

4. Use the secret code to find the summer message.

a	b	c	d	e	f	g	h	i	l	m	n	o	p	r	s	t	w
1	2	3	4	5	6	7	8	9	10	11	12	13	14	15	16	17	18

___ ___ ___ ___   ___ ___ ___ ___   ___ ___ ___ ___   ___ ___ ___ ___ ___   ___ ___ ___ ___ ___
(18)(5)(1)(15)   (6)(10)(9)(14)   (6)(10)(13)(14)(16)   (13)(12)(17)(8)(5)   (2)(5)(1)(3)(8)

Unit 18

Summer Holidays

List Words

- plane
- atlas
- boat
- crab
- passport
- rock
- flipflops
- beach
- flight
- ticket
- runway
- landing
- pool
- hotel
- salty
- uniform
- said
- there

Revision Words

- bucket
- spade
- wave
- site
- seagull
- seaweed
- number
- him

Proofreading

5. Circle the incorrect words and rewrite them correctly in the spaces.

(a) The plain landed on the beech.

_____ _____

(b) Their is a krab in the swimming pole.

_____ _____ _____

Read and Draw

6. He is at the beach with a bucket and spade.

Changing Words

7. Change one letter in each word to make a list or revision word.

(a) these _____   (b) plate _____

(c) cram _____   (d) rook _____

(e) maid _____   (f) lending _____

Compound Words

8. Match the words to make compound words.

(a) run   •   • port

(b) sea   •   • flops

(c) pass   •   • way

(d) flip   •   • gull

Summer Holidays

Unit 18

Word Search

9. Find the list and revision words in the word search.

- plane
- boat
- passport
- flipflops
- flight
- runway
- pool
- salty
- said
- bucket
- wave
- seagull
- seaweed
- him
- number
- atlas
- crab
- rock
- beach
- ticket
- landing
- hotel
- uniform
- there
- spade
- site

More Than One

10. Add 's' or 'es' to make more than one.

(a) beach _____   (b) number _____

(c) atlas _____   (d) plane _____

(e) wave _____   (f) site _____

Additional Activities

11. (a) Write six more 'summer holiday' words. Check your spelling.

(b) Write your new words in alphabetical order.

(c) Write a holiday postcard to your friend. Use all six of your new words.

Difficult Words I Have Found

Word	Practise	Practise	Practise

My Spelling Dictionary Aa to Ff

| Aa | Bb | Cc |
| Dd | Ee | Ff |

My Spelling Dictionary Gg to Ll

Gg

Hh

Ii

Jj

Kk

Ll

My Spelling Dictionary Mm to Ss

Mm	Nn	Oo
Pp	Qq	
Rr	Ss	

My Spelling Dictionary Tt to Zz

Tt

Uu

Vv

Ww

Xx

Yy

Zz